WHAT REALLY HAPPENED?

The True Story of
LEWIS AND CLARK

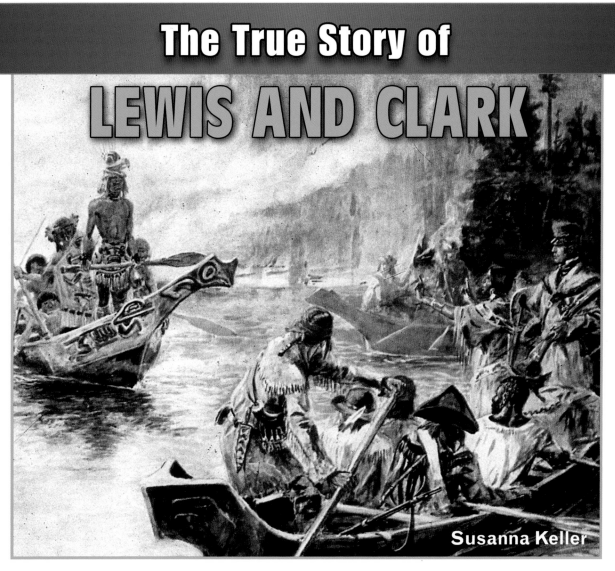

Susanna Keller

PowerKiDS
press.

New York

For Molly, Kevin, and Megan Spring

Published in 2013 by The Rosen Publishing Group, Inc.
29 East 21st Street, New York, NY 10010

First Edition

Editor: Jennifer Way
Book Design: Colleen Bialecki

Photo Credits: Cover, pp. 9, 17 MPI/Stringer/Archive Photos/Getty Images; p. 5 Lewis and Clark with Sacagawea, Paxton, Edgar Samuel (1852–1915)/Private Collection/Peter Newark American Pictures/The Bridgeman Art Library; p. 7 Albert de Brujin/Shutterstock.com; p. 11 David David Gallery/Superstock/Getty Images; p. 13 Richard Cummins/Lonely Planet Images/Getty Images; p. 15 Sacagawea with Lewis and Clark during their expedition of 1804–06, Wyeth, Newell Convers (1882–1945)/Private Collection/Peter Newark American Pictures/The Bridgeman Art Library; p. 19 iStockphoto/Thinkstock; p. 21 Jean-Erick Pasquier/Gamma-Rapho/Getty Images.

Library of Congress Cataloging-in-Publication Data

Keller, Susanna.
 The true story of Lewis and Clark / by Susanna Keller. — 1st ed.
    p. cm. — (What really happened?)
Includes index.
ISBN 978-1-4488-9694-3 (library binding) — ISBN 978-1-4488-9846-6 (pbk.) —
ISBN 978-1-4488-9847-3 (6-pack)
1. Lewis and Clark Expedition (1804–1806)—Juvenile literature. 2. West (U.S.)—Discovery and exploration—Juvenile literature. 3. West (U.S.)—Description and travel—Juvenile literature. 4. Lewis, Meriwether, 1774–1809—Juvenile literature. 5. Clark, William, 1770–1838—Juvenile literature. 6. Explorers—West (U.S.)—Biography—Juvenile literature. I. Title.
 F592.7.K45 2013
 917.804'2—dc23

                                    2012030773

Manufactured in the United States of America

CPSIA Compliance Information: Batch #W13PK4: For Further Information contact Rosen Publishing, New York, New York at 1-800-237-9932

CONTENTS

HISTORY OR STORY?

In 1803, Meriwether Lewis and William Clark set off on one of the most important journeys in American history. They headed west from the eastern United States and kept going until they reached the Pacific Ocean. They learned a lot about the land, wildlife, and Native Americans along their route.

Though the fact that they made this trip is widely known today, people sometimes get confused about some of the details. For example, while the trip is called the Lewis and Clark **expedition**, the pair did not travel alone. There were more than 30 other permanent members of their party, or traveling group. Lewis's dog, Seaman, came along, too!

This picture shows Lewis and Clark with Sacagawea, a Native American woman who joined them partway through their journey.

GROWING UP

William Clark was born on August 1, 1770, in Caroline County, Virginia. When he was young, his family moved to what is now Kentucky. At that time it was the **frontier**. William Clark joined the army at 19 and did well. In 1795, Meriwether Lewis was assigned to serve under him.

Lewis was also from Virginia. He was born on August 18, 1774. Since his father had died when he was young, Meriwether Lewis managed his family's lands from a young age. In 1801, President Thomas Jefferson asked Lewis to be his **secretary**. Lewis moved to Washington, D.C., and began to work at the White House.

While working for Thomas Jefferson, Lewis lived and worked in the White House.

THE LOUISIANA PURCHASE

When Lewis, Clark, and the rest of their party set off to explore the West, they were exploring land that had just become part of the United States. On July 4, 1803, Jefferson announced that the United States had signed a **treaty** to buy the Louisiana Territory from France for around $15 million. The Louisiana Territory covered about 820,000 square miles (2.1 million sq km) of land west of the Mississippi River.

Settlers had been moving west across the Appalachian Mountains to find inexpensive land since the end of the **American Revolution**. Now they would have plenty of room to spread out.

This map shows what the United States looked like in 1803. The Louisiana Purchase doubled the United States' territory.

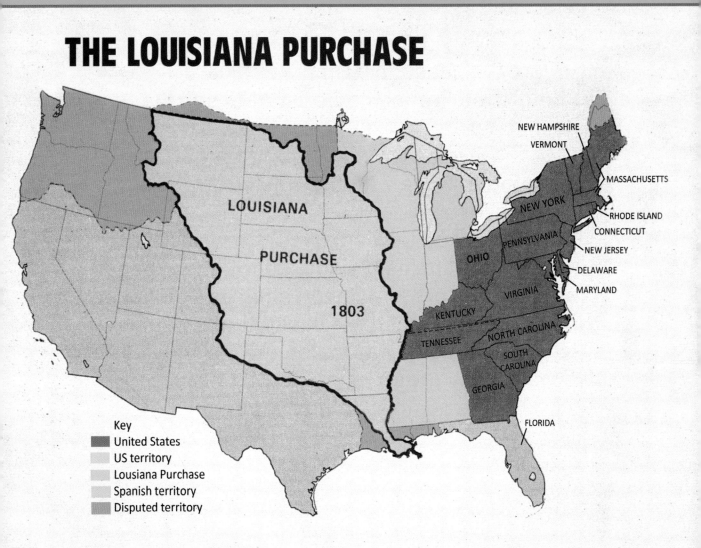

THE LOUISIANA PURCHASE

LOUISIANA

PURCHASE

1803

NEW HAMPSHIRE

VERMONT

MASSACHUSETTS

NEW YORK

RHODE ISLAND

CONNECTICUT

PENNSYLVANIA

NEW JERSEY

OHIO

DELAWARE

MARYLAND

VIRGINIA

KENTUCKY

TENNESSEE

NORTH CAROLINA

SOUTH CAROLINA

GEORGIA

FLORIDA

Key
United States
US territory
Lousiana Purchase
Spanish territory
Disputed territory

GETTING READY

Jefferson asked Congress to fund an expedition to explore the West on January 8, 1803. This was before the French had offered to sell the Louisiana Territory! Americans knew a river route to the Pacific would be good for trade. They also wanted to trade with the western Native Americans for furs.

Jefferson asked Lewis to lead the expedition. Lewis picked Clark as his coleader. Lewis spent several months ordering gear, such as compasses. Lewis and Clark picked the expedition members together. The group was called the Corps of Discovery. This group included Clark's slave, York, who was a full member of the expedition.

The Louisiana Purchase lands that Lewis and Clark were going to explore eventually became part of 15 different states.

HEADING WEST

    Lewis headed west along the Ohio River in late summer 1803. He picked up men and supplies along the way. In October, he met Clark at Clarksville, in what is now Tennessee. They continued down the Ohio River until they reached the Mississippi River. They headed north to St. Louis, in what is now Missouri. They built a winter camp nearby.

    In the spring of 1804, they headed up the Missouri River. They spent the winter of 1804 in today's North Dakota, with the Mandan and Hidatsa Native Americans. Along the way, several people joined the expedition. French Canadian fur traders spoke Native American languages and acted as **translators**.

This is Fort Mandan, where the Corps of Discovery spent the winter of 1804. They left in the spring of 1805 to continue the expedition.

SACAGAWEA

One of the people who joined the expedition was Toussaint Charbonneau. He brought along Sacagawea, one of his two young wives. She was a Shoshone Native American who had been captured by a Hidatsa war party. The Shoshones lived near the **headwaters** of the Missouri River. Lewis and Clark planned to buy horses from them. They planned to use these horses to cross the Rocky Mountains.

On February 11, 1805, Sacagawea gave birth to a son, Jean Baptiste. He came along on the voyage, too. Sacagawea translated when the expedition reached the Shoshones that August. The Shoshone chief they met turned out to be her brother, Cameahwait!

Sacagawea's presence helped the corps in other ways. When Native Americans saw Sacagawea was part of the corps, they viewed the group as peaceful travelers.

O! THE JOY!

A Shoshone guided the expedition across the mountains. It was a hard trip. The **explorers** rested with the Nez Percé Native Americans. Then they headed down the Clearwater River to the Snake River and then the Columbia River. On November 7 1805, Clark famously wrote "O! The Joy!" He believed he had spotted the Pacific Ocean. However, the water he saw was still a part of the Columbia River. On November 15, the expedition reached the ocean.

On November 24, everybody, including York and Sacagawea, voted on where to spend the winter. This was long before African Americans and women got the right to vote. The group voted to build Fort Clatsop, near today's Astoria, Oregon.

This painting shows Lewis, Clark, and the Corps of Discovery meeting a group of Native Americans on the Columbia River in today's Oregon.

DISCOVERIES

   The expedition headed back the following spring. They broke up into groups to cover more ground for a while but regrouped in August. They reached St. Louis on September 23, 1806. They brought many things with them, including maps Clark had made. Lewis brought descriptions of plants and animals unknown in the East and Europe, such as bitterroot, pronghorns, and bison. He even killed and preserved examples.

   In time, other Americans followed in the expedition's footsteps. Americans settled the West, planted farms, and changed the landscape. They pushed many of the native peoples Lewis and Clark had met off their lands.

Lewis and Clark saw bison on the Great Plains. These animals were plentiful there but unknown to people living in the eastern United States.

THE FINAL YEARS

The returning expedition members were celebrated as heroes. Jefferson made Lewis governor of the Louisiana Territory. He then moved to St. Louis, in today's Missouri. Sadly, Lewis died in 1809 while on his way to Washington, D.C. Most **historians** agree that Sacagawea died in 1812. After Sacagawea's death, Clark looked after her children.

Clark married Julia Hancock in 1808. They named their son Meriwether Lewis Clark. Clark had Lewis's **journals** published. He served as the governor of the Missouri Territory from 1813 until 1820. He eventually freed York. Jean Baptiste lived in many places, including Germany and California, before dying, in Oregon, in 1866.

These portraits of Lewis (left) and Clark (right) were done shortly after they had returned from their expedition.

WHAT REALLY HAPPENED?

Since describing their journey was one of the expedition's goals, there are fairly good records of most of the trip. However, for some parts of the journey the records may have been lost or never made. While the Americans wrote what they thought of the Native Americans, the Native Americans left fewer records of their encounters with the corps.

Some people choose to overlook things about the expedition, like the fact that people who disobeyed orders were treated harshly. Other people don't want to admit that it would have failed without Native American help. While the true story is complicated, it is still worth celebrating.

GLOSSARY

American Revolution (uh-MER-uh-ken reh-vuh-LOO-shun) Battles that soldiers from the colonies fought against Britain for freedom, from 1775 to 1783.

expedition (ek-spuh-DIH-shun) A trip for a special purpose.

explorers (ek-SPLOR-erz) People who travel and look for new land.

frontier (frun-TEER) The edge of a settled country, where the wilderness begins.

headwaters (HED-wah-turz) The source of a stream or a river.

historians (hih-STOR-ee-unz) People who study the past.

journals (JER-nulz) Notebooks in which people write their thoughts.

secretary (SEK-ruh-ter-ee) The person who keeps the records for a group.

translators (trans-LAY-terz) People who help people who speak different languages understand each other.

treaty (TREE-tee) An official agreement, signed and agreed upon by each party.

INDEX

WEBSITES

Due to the changing nature of Internet links, PowerKids Press has developed an online list of websites related to the subject of this book. This site is updated regularly. Please use this link to access the list:
www.powerkidslinks.com/wrh/lecl/